A Word in Your Ear

poems

Monroe Spears

Louisiana State University Press

BATON ROUGE

2001

10 09 08 07 06 05 04 03 02 01
5 4 3 2 1

Designer: Amanda McDonald Scallan
Typeface: Sabon
Typesetter: Coghill Composition Co., Inc.
Printer and binder: Thomson-Shore, Inc.

Library of Congress Cataloging-in-Publication Data

Spears, Monroe Kirklyndorf.
    A word in your ear : poems / Monroe Spears.
      p.   cm.
    ISBN 0-8071-2722-1 (cloth : alk. paper) — ISBN 0-8071-2723-X (paper : alk. paper)
    I. Title.

PS3569.P417 W67   2001
811'.54—dc21   2001035714

The author offers grateful acknowledgment to the editors of the following publications, in which some of the poems herein first appeared, sometimes in slightly different form: *Harvard Advocate, Hudson Review, Michigan Quarterly, Mountain Journal, New Review, Sewanee Review, Slant, Southern Review,* and *Striver's Row.*

A limited edition of the poems in the first section was published as *The Levitator and Other Poems* by Pilgrim Press, Princeton, New Jersey, in 1975.

for Betty

Contents

THE LEVITATOR

A WORD IN YOUR EAR

In the little hours, the phone rings,
   loud in the sleeping house.
Once such calls were rare;
   they meant sickness or death.
Now they are still bad news,
   but the voice and the breath
May have found you at random—
   a drunk, adolescent, or warped brown mouse—
Someone who got the wrong number,
   or chose yours for a lark—
And now is suddenly whispering in your ear,
   in bed in the dark.

PAS DE DEUX

The ballerina floats with ease and grace;
Amorous music bears her on its tide;
Her manly partner waits, his feet set wide;
In perfect trust, she leaps; a sure embrace
Receives her; then they move at slower pace;
With loving, clinging gestures like a bride
She wreathes his body's strength, or by his side
Shapes love to music looking in his face.

Backstage, she's horse-faced, duck-butted, hating men,
While he loves nothing else. They hate each other.
Slew-footed monsters, heavy-legged and short, they grin
And mug, sweating. Which of us would not rather
Believe them onstage? Their image there's not false, but twin
To what we all produce: illusion is our mother.

THE LEVITATOR

All I have to do is will it:
I rise gently and float in the air.
Then I move as I wish: sometimes I climb steeply
      or dive,
But most of the time I like to hover, or move
      slowly along
Just clearing the trees and housetops, and looking
      down.

No one else can do this, but I can.
No one knows my secret,
And I am careful never to betray it.
I could astonish everyone, but I never do.

So this dream—for that, of course, is what it is—
Is not just fulfilling the wish to be superior
      (though that may be part of it);
Nor is it simply a disguise for sex:
It feels good, all right, but not that way:
There is no passion or conflict, no building to a climax,
No danger or guilt; instead, a pure and tranquil joy,
A sweetness that comes from feeling at once
      completely free
And completely safe, confident of my own secret
      abilities.

This was never a dream of omnipotent power like
      Superman,
One of my earliest versions came, in fact, from
      Peter Pan:
Like Betty Bronson in that ancient movie
When Wendy blew the moondust on,
I would rise until I bumped the ceiling,
Then swim out of the bedroom window while
      the big dog barked.

But that opening scene was all:
I never had a tribe of Lost Boys, never believed
        in fairies,
And never refused to grow up; in fact, I soon yearned
        to do so,
For war birds in the Lafayette Escadrille had to be
        somewhat older.

Sometimes I flew my Spad right down the highway
        just outside of town
(Where in the daytime I rode my bike down the hill
        to the swimming pool):
Goggled and silk-scarved, I was reckless, doomed,
        and gallant,
And once the war was over, nothing mattered
        anymore.

But this was daydream just as much as nightdream.
So was the boy inventor, saving the world
        from the Martians
With his antigrav machine from *Amazing Stories;*
Both were alibis, explaining why the dreary present
Was so unimportant, compared to exciting pasts
        or futures.

In that drab life of daytime, flying turned out to be
        mostly a bore
(As had making flying objects, whether model planes
        or arrows):
Riding in barnstormers, Ford Trimotors; then, in the
        second war
(Though by then with eyes too dulled by reading to
        be a pilot),
Much flying in many planes. But even jets were too
        awkward and noisy,
And jet belts, when they come, will clearly be the
        same:
My dream will not come true by mechanical
        contrivance.
I want neither speed and power, nor bored monotony.

Once at Salzburg, riding a slow ski lift in summer
Just above the trees, in calm and fragrant silence,
It was almost like the dream, and the only time awake.

So what does the dream mean? Poets no longer
            identify with birds—
Larks and nightingales are out, windhovers and even
            the darkling thrush—
Nor do they soar upward on the winged horse;
But still, there is always a kind of analogy:
Flying must stand for the other gift I wish I had,
With its mastery both of the self and the medium—
To float is to be at peace because fulfilled.

But reading Freud, I find another answer,
And I realize at once that it must be true:
Such dreams, he says, are attempts to recapture
The feeling of being tossed in the air as a small child,
So sure of being supported that one forgets
            the hands that are always there.

The hands that made me fly must have belonged to
The father I have trouble remembering—
Middle-aged at my birth, he was often sick and
            impatient;
When I rubbed his temples, the veins were knotted
            like cords—
They broke when I was twelve, and the world has
            never been the same.

To fly has always meant to defy the established limits
(Though we tend to forget this now as we board
            our jets):
If God had meant us to fly he'd have given us wings;
Disobeying his father's instructions, Icarus fell.

But my happy floating is without fear or guilt.
There is no rebellion; there will be no Fall
(Or if there was, it would be after the days of flying):

So I am no Icarus. As I try to remember
The feeling of floating over supporting hands,
Of daring but riskless feats, venturesome but approved,
Free but part of a larger pattern, weightless and
      guiltless,
At one with myself and my father, united in joy and
      love,

I see that my dream must be also religious:
Like the saints who levitate in rapture, floating
      buoyantly around the garden,
I am glimpsing release from the weight of sin, the
      burden of separateness, the bonds of earth;
I must be yearning for Eden, for lost harmony with
      the Father.

But I don't have the dream much anymore.

TAKE A DIVE

To enter through the mirror
    The ocean in the eye
Requires a plunge down greater heights
    Than any in the sky.

No preparation's needed;
    Prerequisites are none;
But you must trust the air beneath
    And fall true, like a stone.

Must hold the skittering mind
    Hard to the now and here,
Not sliding back to yesterday,
    Forward, or anywhere.

Once fallen, you will make it:
    Immersed in your own depths
Will drown in sweetness, then revive
    And wonder why you slept.

OUT OF CONTROL

Earth-filled, the truck hurtles down the hill.
I hammer on the cab; the burly driver
   Pays no attention. I fear his rage
   More than the coming wreck, and stop.

Water pours and gushes, leaks and drips.
I try frantically to stop it. The faucet turns in my
       hand
   Helplessly; no valves work.
   Meanwhile, the water gushes and pours.

The fire, blown by air, roars higher.
I turn the gascock down, but heat increases.
   Her hair and face grow transparent, as on paper
   Consumed by flames. I wake in horror.

SPECTACLES

Protected by his glasses and his truss
He watched the ugly struggles of the masses;
Not for him, this grunting sweaty muss
Of football games, or chasing after lasses.

Like Harold Lloyd's (though not such obvious fakes)
His glasses put him in another barrel;
But somehow they did not bring him the breaks
That always won the girls and games for Harold.

In later years, no longer Grandma's Boy,
He leered like Bobby Clark or even Groucho;
Witty and randy, rather brash than coy
(Though hardly any desert sheik or gaucho).

Detached observer, though, when things got grim
Remained his role, behind his gleaming lenses;
Eyeball-to-eyeball seemed too crude to him;
He always favored mending walls and fences.

Still looking on, he feels the world pass by
With greater speed now as he grows much older;
Trapped under ice, rolling a frantic eye
At thickening screens that keep him ever colder.

WIND*

The hats are soaring high from the craggy heads of
      the homeowners
In the air there is a sound like screaming
Shingles and tiles are everywhere coming off roofs
And on all the coasts   the papers say   the tides are
      rising

It is stormy there   the wild seas are crouching to
                     spring
   On the land   to devour thick dams and wooded
      ridges

Almost everyone has a heavy cold in the head

The railroad trains are falling from their high bridges

*Based on *Weltende* by Jakob Van Hoddis (1910)

IN TIME

He Is it too late, or will there still be time?
   The light fails, and the summer; coming season
   Of dark and cold before them cast their shadows;
   The boats I've missed, the chances that are passing
   Make desperate my fear of never living,
   Of being left behind in constant changes.

She But what we must learn is to love the changes,
   Not trying either to stand still or outrun time:
   Not building towers to immure us, living
   In which, like princesses, above the seasons,
   We see only through mirrors what is passing,
   For safety's sake condemn ourselves to shadows

   Or, like the motorist, outrun the shadows,
   Studying the road ahead, alert for changes,
   Checking the rearview mirror for cars passing
   But never noticing the inside time:
   An armored space protects both from the seasons
   And cuts them off from contact with the living.
   Instead, we must try now to find the living,
   Not fly away to other worlds of shadows
   Or solid moon, or antique heaven without seasons
   Where treasure could be stored up, safe from changes;
   What other worlds are real, lack human time:
   Our life is always here and now, and passing.

He Yes, we must play our roles in what is passing
   Without apology, take place among the living
   Who weave the patterns of the present time.
   Listen: from over yonder in the shadows
   The string quartet is playing. In music, changes
   Are made as we should make them. Its seasons

   Are wholehearted; they cannot rush or drag like human seasons.
   Heard fully, no repeat can bore while passing,

13

For every moment is unique. No major changes
Can be made in the pattern, yet each point is living
Because they fuse—the players in the shadows—
Join with each other and accept the time.

Both With middle ages, the seasons chill; yet living
With fall ahead and daylight passing, in these shadows
We hear and feel the changes, and we hope in time.

A POET HIDDEN

He always knew at heart he was a poet:
He had a way with language, felt so keenly.
In adolescence he could let verse flow; it
Made Mother proud and thrilled his girls routinely.

But what he wrote was, as he saw too well,
Not really all that good; and so in time
He stopped. The poet's role still cast its spell,
But not hard work on stuff not worth a dime.

So now he finds himself, at forty-odd,
Deciding late that he must face it squarely:
Non-writing poets do not get the nod;
The muse is cold to those who seek her rarely.

Resolving to write each day twenty lines,
He cringes at producing so much junk;
Reminds himself that only thus are signs
Of true ore to be found, unless when drunk.

But no map shows, no chart prepared by sounding,
Where treasure may be buried in his island;
To type his twenty lines, with shoulders rounding,
He slogs through dark, soft swamp and rocky highland.

The search itself, he hopes, may be enough:
The treasure found to be the act of seeking;
So, though he finds the going very rough,
Keeps on the move, techniques and joints all creaking.

Is it enough? You, reader, may decide:
Look hard, like dentist for the signs of caries;
Or go by faith, like Peter Pan's own side:
Applaud to show you do believe in fairies.

BRUTE FACTS

The body hung black in the tree.
Firemen brought ladders, took it off the power line
Charred, tattered, head flopping dreadfully.
I watched from my house across the street the results
      of his climb.
Blond, delicate, and timid . . . we had called him a
      mama's boy,
Only child of middle-aged parents, their anxious joy.

The chicken hung by its feet from the cord.
(I had had to tie it up finally to hit it.)
With my Boy Scout bow, I put arrow after arrow
      into the squawking mess,
But it refused to die, and protesting to the Lord,
The black cook had to be brought out to end
      the nightmare
By wringing its neck as usual—though it flopped
      long without head.

My father lay helpless on the bed.
When the clotted brain-vessel broke, he called, speech
      blurred,
And had lain since panting like an animal, hoarse
      and loud.
My mother wiped his lips and got him fed,
But he knew neither her nor me.
His head was no use to him till the end.

What can we know of death, who have to die?
These three shapes were the first I saw him in.
After the day I saw my father lie
Inhuman as a wax doll, not my kin,
I knew that neither will nor love nor brain
Can save us from grotesque and helpless pain.

Now I am older than my father then
That night he called but could no clear words bring

(Who had been most articulate of men)
Because he had transformed to a thing;
And my time too will come, my head flop broken,
Explaining nothing more, its words all spoken.

Death looms for me since as no grinning skull
But as a twitching carcass, uncontrolled;
As if alive, it flops, its head a null—
Like butcher's meat, though horribly not cold.
The body's half-life: this is what I fear
More than cessation. It grows likelier each year.

A DAINTY FRENCH FORM

What poet can resist a villanelle?
A springing trap, implacable and tight,
It is no scarier than a padded cell.

This kind of place is where we all now dwell,
A form we feel expressive of our plight:
What poet can resist a villanelle?

Our tales are short, and cast their deepest spell
In rigid shapes with lines exactly right;
It is no scarier than a padded cell.

Like Pavlov's dogs we drool at every bell;
No rats are we to dream of taking flight:
What poet can resist a villanelle?

Our doomed world gives off many a gruesome smell;
Our choked skies let in very little light;
It is no scarier than a padded cell.

In earlier times, man stood or else he fell;
But now he seems to pause, transfixed by fright.
What poet can resist a villanelle?
It is no scarier than a padded cell.

TWO DATED OBSERVATIONS
1971

I. News from the Campus

How on earth can one write a light ballad
    In times that are heavy and glum?
Looking back on the days that were salad
    Is one way, quite successful for some;
Or else one may look at the future
    Providing one plays it for laughs:
Not the wound, but the hemstitching suture,
    Not the bomb, but the bright epitaphs.

But the future seems most problematical
    (And not just because of the nukes);
All the trends that were so emblematical
    Have turned out now to be merely flukes:
The teenagers are growing less numerous;
    They will soon cease to dominate styles;
The Chinese have turned courtly and humorous,
    And hard times have come back from the files.

The much-feared population explosion
    Seems to be, after all, just a dud,
Though pollution gets worse, and erosion
    May yet leave us nothing but mud;
While we ride on the moon now, the space flights
    Have diminished in interest and thrills;
Alien life hasn't given the race frights:
    Neither saviors nor monsters with gills.

On the campus, the scene is less populous;
    Demonstrations no longer are in;
Jobs are scarce here, as in the metropolis,
    And budgets are tighter than sin;
The demand for more teachers and scientists
    That we lived with so long is kaput;

Women's Lib comes on here like a lioness,
    But no other such plots are afoot.

Since the birth rate has dropped, marching morons
    May not smother us all in the end,
Though the prospect of opening the door on
    Reproduction by cloning must tend
To produce even more apprehension:
    For who chooses the ones to be cloned?
Will the commune replace single marriage?
    Or will wives be informally loaned?

To such questions as these there's no answer
    Emerging from any machine;
Vietnam still drags on, as does cancer,
    Though some hope for both may be seen;
If there's one thing we've learned that is suitable
    To conclude with (no genial wink)
It is this: that the future's inscrutable:
    What it brings will not be what we think.

Envoy: To Allen Tate

It may seem both absurd and improper
    To address such an eminent bard—
Who in prose is severe as a copper
    And whose verse is miraculous, but hard—
In a style flip and unceremonious;
    But as friend he is gentle and warm,
Un-self-important among his begonias;
    So I send him this galloping form.

II. News from the Barbershop

Playboy these days is bringing into view
The pubic hair and crotch, not just the breasts;
Close-ups of these, of course, are nothing new—
The hard-core mag in them its all invests—

But tit mags, till the very recent past,
Were limited to what's above the waist.

A glimpse, sometimes, of Venus' mount's far slopes—
But shaven clean—so much the constant reader
Might get, to gratify his fondest hopes;
But otherwise the solitary needer
Had to make do with breasts, piquant or large,
In coyly varied poses, for his charge.

Like mermaids were these girls (though their attractions
Comprised no singing, nor much combing hair)
Since of their forms considerable fractions
Remote as fishes' were—though never bare.
Creatures of dream were both—not real life girls—
All outsize breasts, wasp waists, and teeth like pearls.

The new trend took its cue from "adult" cinema
(Made for perennial striplings, as we know):
Those blue films bare and clinical as an enema
In which the crotch is very much on show;
The curious thing is that this new exposure
Makes girls seem people again—and also cozier.

For crotches are not standardized (not yet):
The hair grows as it will, and in this nook
Is neither cut nor dyed nor teased with net;
No fashion dictates how it ought to look;
What thus began as one more form of crudity
Ends by restoring point once more to nudity.

Bunnies in costume all may look alike—
The breasts stuffed out, the fluffy tail at rear—
But real fur, open in the pose they strike,
Is too distinctive to provoke a leer:
For private parts, though publicly displayed,
Reveal one person, strange and oddly made.

Running naked through the forest in the rain—
That's poetry, she said. So female, I thought, her brain—
Lady poets always thinking with their hips—
I smiled, superior; but as I watched the tips
Of green trees blow beyond the rainy glass
Within which we were sheltered, I felt harass
Me the sense that she was right. She might catch cold,
But open to whatever happened, she'd hold
Nothing back, and things would happen. Outside, then,
Is where the poet belongs. Wordsworth, your sin
Was making this view dreary in the extreme; spring woods
Teach nothing of moral evils and of goods,
But they do keep us aware of change and time
And this is what poetry's about. Quicklime
Is closer to the bone than air-conditioned
Stasis under glass. Ripeness is all. Positioned
Inside we may forget our nature; weather
Must be accepted, lived through, not ignored. Leather
Is protection enough against it; armor
Always defeats itself. A wise embalmer
Limits his aims; you gotta go with the flow
The young say now. (Western wind, when wilt thou blow?
They used to say.) Force-fed chicken and beef lacks
Real taste; not only time-snobs, crackpots, and quacks,
But everyone sees now that animals need
To be alive fully, more than free endless feed:
They need weather and running and change. We too
Need these things, must accept, love them, find anew
That being human means to love the weather,
Sharing our common fate, unarmed, together.

I thought all this; said nothing at all. But she
No longer most concerned now with poetry
Was out running through the forest in the rain.

REMEMBERING AUDEN
d. September 28, 1973

I.

Now that a year has passed, it may just be possible:
　　Not an elegy on the great elegist
(Self-defeating as a play on Shakespeare in blank
　　　　verse)
　　But verse about him and—no escaping—me.

My kite has not been flying at all well here lately:
　　It takes hard running to get it off the ground,
And then, most of the time, it comes drifting right
　　　　back down.
　　More tail may be what's needed (kite tail, of course)
For weight and drag, positioning to take up the wind.

But heaviness never helped in dealing with Auden;
　　Lightness, even when feeble, was what he was for.
Loving language, he held anagrams had a meaning:
　　From *Eliot (T. S.)* all you could get was *Litotes,*
He said, and from *Yeats (W. B.)* would have got,
　　　　I suppose, *Best way?*
　　From his own name made this one both funny
　　　　and true:
Why shun a nude tag?

II.

I would welcome his ghost, most generous of
　　　　spirits.
How many writers have truly made friends with
　　　　a critic?
On his last evening with us he sang both *Tristan*
　　　　and *Pal Joey,*
Approved my wife's steak-and-kidney pie, and
　　　　my poems.

Where is he now? Back, let us hope, on the Island
Undisenchanted now, his Staff exhumed, his Book
　　　　salvaged.

Without fear of corrupting, since choice is no longer
        required,
His art can be magic, his love law.

Not as Prospero, but Uncle Wiz—
What exactly does he do?
Surely he dances now when Grace dances,
Corns all cured, bare feet happy in sand.

Here are no flames at midnight, souls arriving on
        dolphins,
Golden birds or drowsy emperors, deathless mouths
        or life-in-death—
Here everyone stumbles bewilderedly out of the sea
And dances in daylight, naked in large white rings.

But there are other occupations: bards recite and
        amiably compete,
Bands play in the limestone landscape, overshot
        waterwheels busily work,
In the evenings there are ballets and operas, much
        singing at all times,
On Sundays, rites but no sermons; choral processions
        on saints' days.

Ariel will have come back (he never wanted to leave)
        for a joyful reunion,
And Caliban as the Flesh is resurrected and improved;
That refined and scrupulous monster will always
        be needed, but now
No longer disturbing, he will flickeringly merge
        with his counterpart.

III.

A tablet now in Poets' Corner
Enshrines him well among his peers;
The Abbey's stone maternal bosom
Forgives the Wanderer's lost years.

In Kirchstetten, a cross remembers
The place his body lies, that once
Pottered about his house, church, village,
Polite to every touring dunce.

Christ Church, his House beloved in Oxford,
Received him back beneath Wren's dome;
In St. Mark's Place (New York, not Venice),
Nothing remains to mark his home.

Who now will translate, hold together
The unwalled City of good will,
Of souls communing in civil joy,
Bodies that dance and eat their fill?

Who now will make Achilles' shield
Or try to bend Ulysses' bow?
The age of heroes having ended,
The Savage God is here below.

Last of the Anglo-American laureates,
Great civilizers, linked with the past,
Who now will praise for us good men and joy in
            life,
Resist the Sirens, still bound to the mast?

IV.

Not reborn in age like Eliot, or raging against it
            like Yeats,
But cheerful, productive, realistic,
Believing at last he would die, apprehensive of
            too much longevity,
He got what he wanted. A coronary, he'd said: It's
            quick and it's cheap.
For him, then, we should rejoice.
                  But for us, it is a different story—
We whose unsecret society is based on knowing our
            weakness,

Who live by faith, not merit, and try to remain human
Still here in the time-bound City
Where the fashionable poets disintegrate like wet
        Kleenex,
Egged on by frustrated prophets to push beyond form,
        even language,
Exploiting their madness or badness, making poems
        of intimate letters
Or suicide (leaving note, "Your move," when jumping
        off bridge)
Open-ended in form and in life, but yearning to close
        both with death.
What are we to do?

V.

St. Wystan was, so his namesake said, dim. (Unilluminatingly martyred for protesting his widowed mother's uncanonical marriage.) The three saints celebrated on September 28 are Eustochium, a Roman virgin, Lioba, an abbess of eighth-century Wessex, and Good King Wenceslas.

So let us consecrate September 28 to St. Wiz.

Over the Feast Day of this doubtful Fish (b. Feb. 21), Zuriel or Uriel, among the angelic orders, will preside.

His emblem is the Island; but in the sea, not a lake.

Generous spirit   now sped forever
Help us to free ourselves   from self-enchantment
Magician who first freed   himself from his spells.

By your strict rules   poets may riddle
Be satiric or comic   but must not curse
May play games   must sing praise
Tell the truth, but not pray   for prayer must
        be prose.

This prayer is unquestionably prose.

Forgive this unmemorable speech.

Blessed Wiz, pray for us.

AUTUMN CONVOCATION

THE OSCILLATOR

Like an enormous tuning fork, the universe oscillates
After each Big Bang—or so some think—
Spreading through space for eons until, like a vast alternating current,
It reverses at last.

B. too oscillates, back and forth, feeling in tune with the universe,
Though up and down (or yoyoing) is his peculiar mode.
    I am a worm and no man—
    But how dare he count me a man like another?
    I am unworthy—but why not the best?

So we all feel sometimes, though in the extreme,
When all connection with the world is lost,
When the swing is from zero to omnipotence,
From being God to being nothing at all,
Then this is madness: manic-depression, they call it
(Or bipolar disorder, in the latest colorless terms).
But B., like most of us, has nothing quite so severe.

No doubt it was the old story:
His mother preferred his father after all.
Poor little B. was crossed in love, will die crossed in love.
It happens to all boys. Why did it damage him so?
Why does he hasten so eagerly
To expose his underbelly to threatening males,
Surrendering, paws in the air, confessing he is always a loser?
(Is he propitiating the father he deeply wishes to kill?)

So once he was rejected, and ever after
Swings wide between the feeling he is worthless
And the secret belief he is superior to all the rest
If only his true worth were recognized.
But, unfortunately, in either case
He remains isolated and alone.

And while he is describing his earlier defeats,
A curious trace of smugness begins to appear,

A suggestion of true worth passed over—
    A mad world, my masters! If things were as they should be
    Then we know who would be on top!
And what he really believes soon appears:
He alone has been virtuous while the rascals have got ahead.
He is superior after all.

Groucho put it perfectly: Why, I wouldn't dream of joining
Any club that would admit people like me!

Is it worse for Americans than others?
Indians or Europeans inherit a fixed place:
They do not expect, on the whole,
To have lives very different from their fathers'.
But we Americans are committed to the future,
To pulling ourselves up by our own bootstraps,
Believing anything is possible for the man who works hard:
You are what you think you are;
You can do whatever you believe you can do.
So why not the best? Every man a king, or imperial president!
Use the secret powers of your own mind!
Find the diamonds in your own backyard!
Make millions in your spare time!
Teach yourself in ten minutes a day!
Dare to be rich! You deserve it!

So most of us, sooner or later, are disappointed:
Our unlimited needs and expectations are not met.
But our friend here is a special case.
B. carefully makes certain his own defeat,
No doubt unconsciously, but against the national credo
That winning is everything. He wants a *moral* victory.

A HORROR STORY

The world around me seems to be growing larger.
All distances are longer, everything I lift is heavier.
The whole universe is expanding, I know, but the red shift in stars
Is not what troubles me. Can it be
That I am shrinking?

It's like growing up, but in reverse, and faster.
In the long days of childhood, with infinite slowness the world began to
shrink
Until, full-grown at last, I found the rooms and furniture and sidewalks
So vast and intimidating in childhood
To be now ridiculously small, touchingly easy to master.

But now it's turning around again. I am not what I was.

What should I do? Call a shrink? What I need is an unshrink.
If I could only find a bottle, as Alice did,
To stop the process. But the bottles I find
Labeled *Drink Me* stop nothing, though they help forget.
Whiskey is not an effective giant-killer.
But (with a bow to Joyce)
The children may as well play, since
The ogre will come in any case.

The Incredible Shrinking Man became a mouse-sized creature
And went in terror of his cat. Domestic coziness
Turned monster, and was out to get him.
I suppose, like him, I'll shrink until at last I disappear.

Isn't that, in fact, what does happen to us all?
We become dimmer and grayer, and gradually,
Like Tithonus, dwindle to nothing but a voice.
And then that goes too.

ACADEMIC DISTINCTIONS

To be a Distinguished Professor, one must insist upon distinctions:
I am not like you, says his apotropaic gesture
(Is it enough to turn away the head?):

> *I have never been one of the crowd.*
> *I have always refused to see myself*
> *In those who compete or follow; I have kept my distance.*
> *My golden vanity is still afloat.*

> *Whatever I am, I am not like those others.*
> *But then, what am I?*

Meditating on this, he feels the ground shift,
Like Dante climbing on Satan's hairy belly,
Down through the center of the world, until down becomes up;

And he finds that he is no longer interested in distinctions.

Crude, stupid, haphazard life has no time for them, he sees.
His own egotism appears as fatuous as Landor's,
Who strove with none for none was worth his strife.
To his surprise he begins to find meaning
In those Eastern affirmations that somehow All Is One,
That beggar and king, wise man and fool, are somehow all the same,
That ambition is unwise, achievement meaningless,
Being part of a larger pattern completed in other lives.

So now he no longer wants to be distinguished.

> *Instead, I want to see myself in others and others in me.*
> *It's not the differences but what we share that interests me now.*
> *As we age we go back to the poor bare forked animal;*
> *All old men are dirty, like all babies.*
> *The dikes break, flooding the Apollonian self*
> *So long cultivated with such care*
> *In the sea of the all-too-human.*

We've been taught not to be common or dirty,
Turn our toes out when we walk, and remember who we are!
But it's back to the dirt we must go.
And under it. And become it.

STORMS

Howling and screaming, intruding under the door,
The wind will never learn good manners.
It rattles the windows, pushes through the weatherstrips.
Its chill factors defeat our insulation.

A thunderstorm can undo us, or storm of snow or ice.
When lightning strikes and trees and power lines go down,
When the lights and furnaces go out and no appliance works,
We huddle in the primitive cave, helpless as our forefathers.

In hurricane season, warned of tropical storms or tornadoes,
Our only defense is flight. As we board up and leave
We realize how puny we are. Sometimes we can tack into the wind,
Sail close to it, work with it in windmills or ships,
But we know who is in command.

A DREAM

Ruggieri's Castle of philosophy . . .
I'm late; that's where I am supposed to be.
People suggest I try another street.

If I should find it, whom would I there meet?
The well-gnawed traitor frozen in Dante's Hell?
Or Roger the dodging lodger, who ends all messages well?

THE SHEPHERD'S COMPLAINT

Academic Variations on a Theme from Auden

But here no nymph comes naked to the youngest shepherd. . . .
I wonder where they do. In daydreams, wet nightdreams, Greek myths—
As the youngest shepherd in this department, I can identify with Paris,
But I don't need three naked goddesses to choose from,
Nor Helen either. I know my limitations.
Just one ordinary nymph-next-door would be fine, thank you.
　　　　　　Once everything seemed possible. When I was very young
I swam in a millpond with two laughing girls
Floating like water lilies in the stream
Inside high wooden walls, in a cold, swift current.
　　　　　　White flesh gleamed under bluegreen water;
Nothing was clear or distinct, not shapes or colors or feelings—
All was blurred and cold and exciting
And anything might happen
With those laughing and lovely girls I hardly knew
Drifting with me, pulled together by the cold flow,
Touching and kissing and laughing
Round and round in the millrace, inside the high wooden walls.
Those girls were nymphs. They might come naked to my bed—
But, of course, they didn't. And here am I, the youngest shepherd,
Grading freshman themes, and knowing very well
Ralegh's "Nymph's Reply." Still, that girl in the back row . . .

But here no nymph comes naked to the youngest shepherd. . . .
The typical narcissistic fantasy of a self-pitying adolescent.
What would he do if one did? An actual girl, in the flesh,
Would be a sad disappointment compared to the perfect glamor
(Produced by trick photography) that is the basis of his dream.
A real girl would have flaws, and her own desires and opinions.
She wouldn't disappear afterwards; there she would be to be dealt with.
Something would have been begun, to continue and somehow end.
There might be problems first with the act of love itself.
In dreams, of course, there are none; but in real life,
With an inexperienced boy, clumsy and overeager—
Well, many nymphs are departed, and
Departing, have left no addresses.

But here no nymph comes naked to the youngest shepherd. . . .
No? If teachers are shepherds and students are sheep,
I'm not so sure: I know quite a few shepherds who
(As the cattlemen crudely put it) have sheepshit in their boots.
These were not nymphs, of course, but poor little lambs who had lost their
       way.
But there was Vanessa, though Swift refused her at last; and Heloise,
Though what happened to Abelard was hardly a happy ending.
Nympha fly slowly from the young entomologist,
And even a middle-aged Humbert sometimes nets his Lolita.
So it can happen, but hardly here, and certainly not to me:
Nobody at all has come stalking within my chamber
With naked foot, or anything else, for a very long time.

But here no nymph comes naked to the youngest shepherd. . . .
Nymph? What do you mean, nymph? A woman is a person,
Not merely a sex object, a creation of male fantasy.
What do you suppose a nymph does when she's not inhabiting dreams?
I am not a nymph, nor a sheep either;
I am as human as you are, and at least as real.
Don't you see that what you want is self-contradictory?
How can the nymph come naked, but only to you?
In real life, only a whore or a very sick girl would do such a thing.
I thought such dreams went out with James Bond and the private eyes,
But I suppose the adolescent mind will always be with us,
Pimply, drooling, pawing the centerfold.
Even past adolescence, most males seem to find women interchangeable:
One nymph is just as good as another; in the dark all cats are gray.
The dog in the manger, the big bull with all the cows—
That's what you all really want.
Well, it's about time we got out of the barnyard.

But here no nymph comes naked to the youngest shepherd. . . .
Well, I, for one, am glad. I can't bear those awful female breasts.
What I've always preferred, more or less secretly,
Is the ephebe, with the love that dare not speak its name,
Though these days it does dare, with reasonable caution; the closet door is
       almost open.
For it's a grand tradition, coming down from Plato

And from centuries of educational experience, that the only good
    pedagogue
Is the one who *loves* his students. Ideally, he loves only their minds,
But there's always been a good chance that bodies won't get left behind.
When Alcibiades crept naked under Socrates' cloak, he was surprised when
    nothing happened,
And not all teachers are Socratic. So what's all the fuss?
Just keep those nymphs away from me, with their soft, jiggly bodies
And silly giggly minds.

But here no nymph comes naked to the youngest shepherd. . . .
Nor, it goes without saying, to the oldest. If one did
She would want to tell him her troubles, seek his advice.
Even naked in bed, she'd talk to him like an uncle.
If she did want more than talk, which is most unlikely,
He is not too sure he could cope; his faith in miracles has waned:
In his cool pastoral, he'd have to play Silenus among the satyrs.
Full of self-pity, he weeps for his vanished youth.
But then he comes to himself. Any possible She
Would approach him as part of the power-structure,
Would want something, would think at the very least that he might be
    useful.
So even if the impossible happened, he would have to pretend it hadn't:
Refuse the offer, say (without using the words) thanks just the same,
I can't take a bribe, abuse a trust, exploit a special relation.
Damn. Oh, well, it won't happen anyway. And things are rough all over.

But here no nymph comes naked to the youngest shepherd. . . .
Isn't that the girl from the back row, waiting outside his office?
She's wearing a black raincoat, and apparently nothing else.
Why is she here?
For her own reasons, no doubt: not just for his pretty blue eyes—
Getting revenge or buying favor, transference working like mad—
But maybe, also, just possibly, love?
When miracles happen, we must believe them.
Here she is, naked and loving.
The Muse visits whom she will.

A PAINFUL SUBJECT

I. Metamorphosis

When Gregor Samsa woke to find himself transformed,
He seemed to be a large disgusting insect.
I wake daily to a more gradual transformation,
Not into bug, but something equally strange and repellent,
A metamorphosis more chilling than any in Ovid.
Girl into tree or star or spider, man into stag or flower,
Strange life flowing in the veins instead of blood,
This is exciting, fascinating; and even better
Stones into men, statues into living girls.
Joyce's characters seem not to mind their endless process
Flowing as they talk into rivers or hills or mythical types.
But my transition seems to be endless and painful both.
Like Gregor, I become less than human,
Possibly smelly or unpleasant,
To be hustled out of sight as quickly as the humans can arrange it.
To go from adult to old man
Is truly to change into another species,
Apart as a lame duck, having no space in the future.

II. Palindrome

Though we have known, at least since Heraclitus,
That the way up and the way down are one and the same,
It is not often noted that there is also
Between growing up and growing old a surprising symmetry.
After sixty, as before fifteen, one's age is public knowledge
And counted in public even to fractions of a year.
One is preoccupied with sight and hearing and bodily functions.
In spite of fear of falling,
The basic accomplishment of walking looms large and precious.
Sleep and food must be just right, and strength not overtaxed.
The adult's sense of mastery, competence, being in control

Becomes a memory. It is almost like
Reversing a film, or reversing any event in Newtonian physics,
Except that it isn't funny.

III. Haydn Old, or The Joy of Aging

Unlike many a genius, Haydn was beloved:
Generous to his rivals, faithful to his wife,
Religious, hard-working, charitable, and kind,
A great artist and a truly good man.

But he lived too long. After *The Seasons*
He recognized that his seasons were finished:
Nothing but winter now; no more rebirths.
But the spring stirrings were still there;
Ideas pursued him "to the point of torture,"
Though he no longer had strength to work them out
Or even write them down. *The Seasons* finished me, he said.

What do you do after you've written *Hamlet?* Well,
If you're Shakespeare you write *Othello, Lear,* and *Macbeth.*
But even for Shakespeare, the question keeps coming up
And eventually there's no answer. He retired, of course,
But even after *The Tempest,* that greatest farewell to the stage,
He couldn't really leave it alone.
In his last years he had a hand in some truly dreadful hackwork.

Faulkner, when at last he won fame and money,
Faced two decades of declining powers.
Einstein, early honored, lived forty years in frustration,
Rejecting the quantum, pursuing the unified field.
After dazzling early success, Rossini spent forty years
Composing only a little church music.
Hawthorne spent his later years trying to write novels
That came apart in his hands.

Why can't the artist break his staff and drown his book?
Does he need his art long after it needs him?

VIER ERNSTE GESÄNGE

I. Academic Nightmare

Mouth and eyes stuffed with chalk dust,
Unable to see, unable to speak

Even if I could find the classroom and remember my subject,
How could I teach?

What every lecturer most deeply fears:
Loveless dust in the eyes and mouth.

What we want is to nourish and fertilize,
To be a source, and perhaps make a modest display.

So, if I must be a clod
Let me dissolve in water,

Or better, let me *be* water,
My fine spray dissolving in air.

If I waste my sweetness on the desert
I'm not really a rose anyway,

But as to pearls and swine
I do have some cultured pearls to offer the sweathogs.

Well, I confess I have always liked academic humor.
Good-bye, Dr. Dryasdust, and thanks.

Let the fountain be my emblem.
Let me not dry up.

II. The Third Ashram

As I approach the border
Of this strange country
Known only from maps,

Where I will go into the forest
Alone, with no company and no possessions,

I say farewell without regret
To my family, my job, and my world,
Knowing that now
My true journey is inward.

When I wake in the morning I will look for water
And for a neem twig to brush my teeth
(It will be hard on the bridgework)
If I am lucky. There won't be any drink before dinner,
Nor any dinner, beyond the odd leaf, root, or berry
(Organic all the way),
And no evening news except the coming of darkness,
Which will be news enough.

III. Security

Everything seemed to be going according to plan.
We followed Poor Richard's advice on how to succeed.
We were fighters and never quit.

But where's the happy ending, the final disclosure
That all our fears were based on misunderstandings
To be cleared up amid happy laughter?

Are things going to keep on getting worse and never get better?
Is there never going to be a satisfactory explanation?
Is this all there is?

If we live long enough, will we find ourselves back in childhood?
When the time comes and we have run out of excuses,
Must we say good-night while the grown-ups laugh and talk
And be put to bed in the dark alone?

IV. To the Reader

Dear gentle reader, why are you reading this?

Are you a frustrated housewife, bored with your businesslike husband,
Dreaming like Emma Bovary, reading in bed?

Or perhaps that husband himself, browsing at newsstand or club,
Picking up this by mistake, looking for sexier amusement?

A dim little gray-haired lady? A yearning adolescent girl?
A pimply-faced youth, poor but earnest, ready for serious debate?

Of course not. You, thank God, are none of the above.
You are a real person, not a stereotype out of fiction,

And I think I know very well why you are here.

You are lonely, like me. Isn't that so? Like me
You would like to understand yourself and your life,
You would like to know what it all means and what you should do.

Well, for the last need you must go to your guru or priest,
But I can, if you will accept me, help with the first:

Believe me real, and you will see yourself in me.
This living hand—see, I hold it toward you—

Forget that Keats said it first, and take it.
Now we are no longer alone.

AGAINST COMMITMENT

While you debate which breeches leg goes first,
Said Johnson, another boy has put on both
And you stand still; sir, meanwhile your breech is bare.

To win, Coach said, you got to really want it.

But I'm not sure at all I really want it,
And if my breech is open to the breeze,
Like Pangloss' wife I'll stand half-assed, undaunted,
Until I find what locks will fit my keys.

If nothing ever fits, those keys will dangle
Forever on the wall, and rust unused;
Better to wait than push and force and mangle
For action's sake, to prove that I can choose.

For Johnson also thought it didn't matter
Which shoe went on which foot; while any clod
Whose feet hurt knows that's madder than a hatter.
The Great Cham sometimes could be very odd.

ACOUSTIC ISOLATION

Smiling and nodding, I pretend that I understand.
Why do they mumble so? Why can't they speak up?
Of course, I know that the trouble is in my own ears.

Heard melodies are sweet, but those unheard
Are sweeter yet—or so I keep telling myself.
But they sound only in the inner ear.
No one else can share this solitary and isolated music.
And most deaf people, judging by their expressions,
Hear little of such inner harmonies.

Beethoven was no smiler. Milton was solemn too
But lacked the fearsome scowl: To be blinded by excess of light
Is dazzling but has its rewards. Blindness once was thought
A divine punishment, often compensated by the gods:
Insight was believed routinely to arrive,
If nothing more, when outsight was lost.

But for deafness, no reimbursement was thought necessary:
The deaf man was lucky if allowed to survive.
"In the early ages the deaf were regarded as idiots
And killed out of hand."

So no doubt I should rejoice that things are as they are:
We no longer throw the stragglers to the wolves
Or abandon the aged on an ice floe.
But we can't make them once more members of the pack.
If you can't hear the drum, you can't march with the others.

To be marooned is better, though, than drowning.

EYE AND EAR

Beg pardon? I didn't quite catch that.

To be blind is, often, to be gentled,
To accept the loss through its varied compensations:
The inner life enriched by the affliction,
The disposition sweetened; for the deeper senses—
Smell, taste, touch, hearing—become stronger and sharper
When sight is removed, with its constant distraction,
Its superficial turmoil.
The blind sink deeper within themselves,
Are more concentrated and still, more intensely aware.

The deaf man, though, can accept nothing.
And there are no compensations. Though his loss is invisible,
He is always aware of what he is missing.
Forever out of it, dead to casual comment or intimate whisper.
Nuances and overtones are lost forever.
Everything has to be repeated and explained to him.

His own voice loud because he cannot hear himself,
He makes others raise their voices, speak loudly and slowly;
Compelled to sound angry and irritable, brusque, argumentative,
They begin to feel that way toward him,
If he tries to conceal his loss, as inevitably he will,
He provokes irritation far more than sympathy.
His interior life grows poorer, not richer.

When he can't hear the voices, man will always feel
Abandoned by his gods.

Eye loves to be tricked, delights in it for hours:
The hand is quicker than the eye—
Now you see it, now you don't.
It is not what you thought—look!
Movies depend on this, and trompe l'oeil paintings
(Mirrors and windows, hands or fruited vines

Coming over the painted frame). Magical illusions—
Ladies floating in air or sawn in half—
The whole art of chiaroscuro, the fascination of the crepuscular,
The half-seen apparition, the teasing glimpse or misty epiphany.

But hearing, or half hearing, is no joke.

Ear is hard to deceive, and hates it:
To be confused by sound,
Not know what it is and where it comes from,
This is unbearable. Ear delights in subtle discriminations,
Enjoys the smallest variations in the patterns it looks for,
Remembers, anticipates, lives in time. But it is defenseless
When confronted by excessive or incoherent sound:
Lacking earlids or nictitating membranes, it cannot shut it out,
And noise can kill or drive insane.

Who can compare losses, or would want to?
As frivolous as arguing that one sense is nobler than the other.
Let me not lose the visible world, with the world of books,
Nor the world of music, at once intimate and noble,
Until at last all losses come together.

THE SHAPE OF MIDDLE AGE

Maurice Chevalier said it: Growing old isn't so bad
When you consider the alternative.

But it is. The homeowner discovers
That the things he thought he owned were only loaned him;
That the only truly private enterprise is dying.
After Making It, he discovers how it comes unmade.

Now that the end of my life is undeniably in sight,
I look back and forward, and wonder what shape it will make.

The worst woud be a zero. Zilch. Not only for total meaning
But because, once past the middle, it's all downhill:
Everything that went up comes down, in a smooth, inexorable curve.

The best would be an hourglass, or a pair of wings:
Either would mean that things will be better:
That the pinched middle I'm in will open out once more.

But what I see is no shape, but a picture:
Myself walking down endless corridors
With closed doors, growing more and more panicky
As I realize I'm lost and won't find the right one.

Or I walk down a city street at night,
Looking across broad sidewalks at massive windows,
Seeing the warm golden glow around the rich drapes
Pulled tight against the dark and cold outside,
And imagine the witty and beautiful people inside
Whom I will never know.

Be creative! we tell our children. Dance! Sing!
    Smear your fingerprints anywhere! Don't be intimidated!
    Nothing is sacred! Nothing is forbidden!
    The walls of the museums have all been removed,
    The audience has been invited onto the stage and into the sanctuary.
    The barriers are down, and art and life never more will be separated.
    For art is only whatever we designate as art:
    The toilet seat hung on the wall, the random sounds from radios,
    The paint dripped from a bucket, any joke or process
    As long as it's joyful and expresses the real you.

But of course we don't really tell them that. It's only the more naive
    Of the ed-psych teachers and the pop-psych exploiters
    Who preach that gospel unchanged. The rest of us want a little quiet
    And an introduction to work, and perhaps a little respect;
    And all this talk about joy makes us slightly uneasy.
    We want them to be happy, of course, but we feel they'd better be
        prepared
    In case things turn out for them as they did for us.

We wonder, too, if joy is really the word for art.
    Even cooking and sex
    And stitchery and whittling and macrame can get boring,
    And it's only best-selling authors who tend to look happy:
    The greater they are, in general, the grimmer they look
    (Think of Shakespeare and Milton, Faulkner, Dante, Beethoven—
    Not a smile among them), and from what we know of their lives,
    Few artists have been very joyful human beings.
    There must be something to hurt them into creating to start with—

And the satisfactions their art provides don't seem to last.
    Most are small or ugly, lame or blind or crippled,
    Sick or crazy or drunk. No, strength through joy won't do.
    Tragic joy is more like it, as in Nietzsche or Mann or Yeats—
    But this isn't what the fingerpainters mean.

What does the artist do when he isn't creating?
    Well, he appears
    Mostly to worry about what, if anything, he will create next
    And sometimes about whether his last work was really any good.
    Everything has its price, and the price of art remains high.

THE HOMEOWNER'S CONFESSION

I have always loved houses and staying safe inside them.
I spent my childhood reading, with the odd glance outside
From windowseat or screened porch. And even in the stories
What I liked best was the cozy, serene time
Before the adventures began, or after they had ended.
(Bless my white spats, said Mr. Damon; Tom, weren't we lucky!)

I know, of course, that neither a physical house
Nor the house of fiction (nor of any other art)
Provides a lasting refuge.
There is no escape from life, no security against change and chance and
     danger:
Door-peekers and double locks will not protect the homeowner,
Nor parents the child, nor art the constant reader—or the writer.

Yet even now I find the dream seductive, bolstered as it is
By the real estate and insurance and home-improvement industries:
Make your home invulnerable with burglar bars, alarm systems, locks and
     chains!
Purchase peace of mind! Protection for the golden years! Safety for your loved
     ones!

It is good for me, then, to live in Houston, where everything is temporary
And NASA already a deserted village. Houses here are built on sand, not rock.
Under the cracked concrete slabs, the sand shifts and subsides.
Air conditioning roars defiance at the heat,
But flash floods and hurricanes intrude at will.

Downtown is a fantasy of skyscrapers, but as for houses,
Except for absurd imports—French châteaux, Tudor half-timbers,
New England salt boxes—
There is one story and one story only; nor do cellars, basements, or attics
Make sense in this flat, swampy land. There is only the odd cathedral ceiling.

Keine feste Burg ist unser Haus—
Long after the Faith ceased to be our fortress
It remained a ramshackle but comfortable roof over our heads.
But now there is only the blinding empty sky.

Of course, it was never really a refuge:
No church can protect, nor house nor cave nor castle.
They cannot even be owned: a house is loaned to us briefly
Then passes to another tenant, unless we destroy it first.

If the childhood dream could come true, that would be the worst horror:
To be reduced at last to a patient or a child again,
Managed, bullied, humored with professional briskness
By a substitute mother. A house is not a womb:
Returning to the nursery is the saddest end of all.

A VALEDICTION: PERMITTING MOURNING

Farewell, large-chested Martians,
      We now, alas, must say;
The thin air of your planet
      Supports no life today;
For since the *Mariner* reports
      It has been sadly clear
No great brains brood in ancient courts
      In that red glowing sphere.

Lunarians or stone Sentries
      Were nowhere on the moon.
We found no secret entries
      There with far worlds in tune;
No alien race in buried mines
      Or with fantastic gear
Left messages or any signs
      That life exists elsewhere.

Alone, then, in the universe,
      Unique, it now would seem,
We have no wise and kindly nurse
      Or nightmare foe to dream;
Our blue and watery planet floats
      Sky's ever-fruitful wife
Among dead or volcanic motes
      Lacking precarious life.

Should planets orbit other stars
      (Though none have yet been seen)
They might contain our avatars
      Under a friendly queen.
But signals have yet to appear
      From silent space around,
And distances too great to bear
      Would separate our ground.

Farewell, then, to such dreaming
       We now, alas, must say;
We loved their pretty scheming;
       Our landscape now is gray;
Banished with elves and fairies,
       UFOs, BEMs, and ETs,
Survive where nothing ever varies,
       In nursery-land movies.

And still, like Bishop Corbet, we
       Mourn their departure too;
We hate the kind of mind that thinks
       It knows what can be true;
That banishes myth and half-belief
       And leaves no mysteries—
Nothing beyond terrestrial grief
       And hopeless histories.

VARIATIONS *SÉRIEUSES*

Et in Arcadia Ego. . . .
I, too, have been in Arcadia. Yes, even I,
Dr. Dryasdust. Once I was young like you;
I was adored once too, and have heard the chimes at midnight.
Once this dry stick was full of sap, alive and open to the rain,
Illuminated by lightning. But that was long ago.

Et in Arcadia Ego. . . .
And once I was in Arcadia. When we alumni
Return to the campus each year at homecoming
(To find each time that you can't go home again)
For one more glimpse of that sweet paradise
Now barred by angels with the flaming sword of age,
Where once all was simple, love was innocent,
Everything was possible, because we all were young—
That was the land of lost content, now gone forever,
And now there's no returning. And it's all downhill.

Et in Arcadia Ego. . . .
Even in Arcadia there is no escape from me.
I am the skeleton at the feast, the bony intruder
Whom you see peering from behind a tree or over a wall
In Renaissance art, to remind you of death.
I am the ultimate bridegroom; my wooing is irresistible
And I get all the girls in the end, whatever the competition—
The cheerleader, Miss Congeniality, Miss Brain,
The ice princess in her high tower, and the girl next door—
They all wind up in my arms.
I am the worm in the apple, the flaw in the eye,
The gray in the golden hair, the sag and wrinkle in the skin.
Time drives the flocks from field to fold, and I,
Least passionate of shepherds, always win.

Et in Academia Ego. . . .
Yes, Academia is our contemporary version of the pastoral myth,
Based, like Arcadia, on real places, but equally remote from them.

As the lives of the real Arcadians in their harsh mountains
Must have been hard and monotonous, nasty, brutish, and short,
So our huge multiversities, producing with absolutely no nonsense
Well-trained MBAs, EEs, Doctors of Administrative Science,
Animal Husbandry, Decision Making, and Alternative Lifestyles,
Bear little resemblance to their myth: communities of scholars
United by humane and religious convictions, wise and kindly,
Unworldly, devoted to truth and the welfare of students—
Who are, themselves, not quite the dear innocents
They will think themselves to have been
Singing nostalgically of bright college years, golden and brief—
And yet the myths are not simply lies. Consider the alternative:
Without these images for models, would we not be impoverished?
Like other visions, these give us hope.

Et in Academia Ego. . . .
I suppose the Academy has been Arcadia for me.
I've spent most of a long life there, quite happily,
And now it is almost time to leave.
Whatever its faults, it's been a fascinating world;
I'm grateful to have been part of it,
And I've loved almost every moment.

But now, though it hasn't changed, I have:
Non sum qualis eram, as Horace memorably put it.
So, Venus, get yourself another boy. Minerva too.
Go and bother the young. I've had it.
It's time to pass on both torches
To those whose grasps are stronger and more—grasping.
Ev'n in our ashes live their wonted fires. . . .
But, traveler, you need shed no tear for me
Nor pause for tribute. I have had my reward.

AUTUMN CONVOCATION

Retired now, I live high on the edge of a mountain.

Standing on my bluff, like a good gambler,
Or a Welsh bard summoning up the whirlwind,
I look down on the valley and call up spirits.
Only the leaves answer, whispering and dry.

But ghosts of other convocations
Stir in my head, and I can make them walk.
Here comes the academic procession.

Marching like summer soldiers, costumed like medieval monks,
And embarrassed by both resemblances, the faculty gets underway
Processing to Brahms, whose academic festival is very short on joy.
Bassoons burbling, brasses braying, horns hoarse and breathy,
Just on the edge of self-parody, here we go again.

Gaudeamus igitur, juvenes dum sumus—
Rejoice let us therefore, young while we are—
Those of us who are not so young feel more and more remote
From the fresh new faces that appear each autumn
Dependably as flowers in spring. Barbarous in beauty,
Here they come again, the vigorous young. But as for me,
I decline with the mellowing year. Decline along with me,
While grades and prices rise.

Some of us see ourselves as Guardians of the Word,
Others as brave explorers on the far frontiers of knowledge;
Some as selfless scientists, keeping the eye on the object,
Others as dedicated radicals, undermining society for its own good,
Emancipating our students from provincial morals and bourgeois ideology.
Some, I fear, are petty tyrants, Professor Unruh or Dr. Dryasdust.

But considering the alternatives, we are not so bad:
Compared to the "real" world (though we eagerly confess our unreality)
The academy smells almost like a rose.

Do I miss it? Would I go back to it
(Considering that a certain convocation of politic worms
Is the only other convocation I shall certainly attend)?
No. I have had my world as in my time;
I am a part of all that I have met;
I belong to my history, and would not live another if I could.
I say without regret, Let go, farewell.

Smiling, I see my ghostly procession dance
As the leaves dance in the wind, accepting their fate and the season.